About This Issue Guide

The immigration issue affects virtually every American, directly or indirectly, often in deeply personal ways. This guide is designed to help people deliberate together about how we should approach the issue. The three options presented here reflect different ways of understanding what is at stake and force us to think about what matters most to us when we face difficult problems that involve all of us and that do not have perfect solutions.

The US government essentially shut down immigration, at least temporarily, during the coronavirus pandemic. But as our country begins to reopen, difficult questions remain:

- Should we strictly enforce the law and deport people who are here without permission, or would deporting millions of people outweigh their crime?

- Should we welcome more newcomers to build a more vibrant and diverse society, or does this pose too great a threat to national unity?

- Should we accept more of the millions of refugees and asylum seekers fleeing gang violence and war, or should we avoid the risk of taking in people whose backgrounds may not have been fully checked?

- Should our priority be to help immigrants assimilate into our distinctively American way of life and insist they learn English, or should we instead celebrate a growing mosaic of different peoples?

The concerns that underlie this issue are not confined to party affiliation, nor are they captured by labels such as "conservative" or "liberal."

The research involved in developing the guide included interviews and conversations with Americans from all walks of life, as well as surveys of nonpartisan public-opinion research, subject-matter scans, and reviews of initial drafts by people with direct experience with the subject.

Immigration

Who Should We Welcome? What Should We Do?

FOR CENTURIES, people from other countries have come to the United States in search of a better life. The steady influx of newcomers helped build the US, creating a mix of cultures, religions, and ethnicities not found anywhere else in the world. Today, people born in another country make up almost 14 percent of the US population.

Before the pandemic overshadowed most other concerns, many people were asking questions about this country's immigration policies, brought to their attention by the recent crises on our southern border and the sharpening debate over border wall construction. As we begin to think about what changes we may want to make, it's helpful to consider where we are now:

How many immigrants are coming into the United States?
Over the last decade, the United States legally accepted about one million immigrants a year. That number was already projected to drop under new policies—put in place before the pandemic border closures— that ban travel from about a dozen countries, cap the number of refugees we will accept, and bar those who will need public benefits.

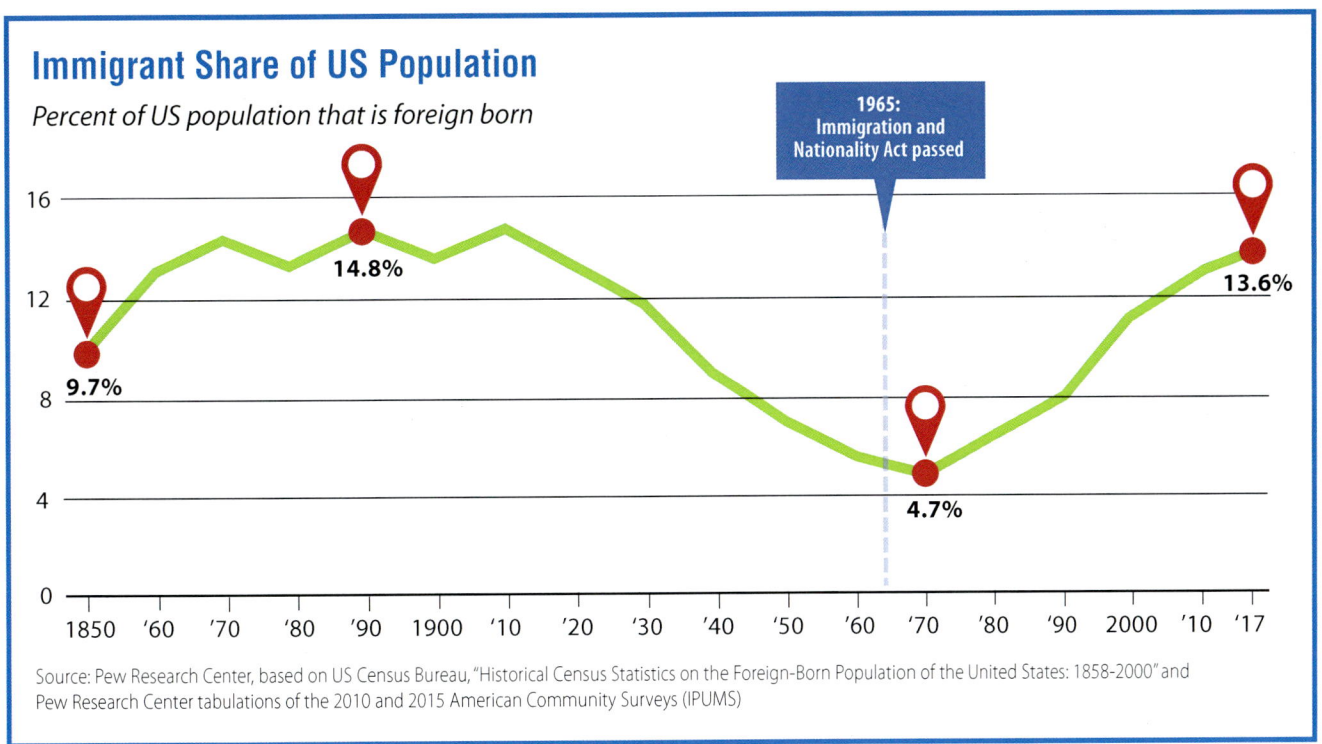

Immigrant Share of US Population
Percent of US population that is foreign born

1965: Immigration and Nationality Act passed

9.7%

14.8%

4.7%

13.6%

Source: Pew Research Center, based on US Census Bureau, "Historical Census Statistics on the Foreign-Born Population of the United States: 1858-2000" and Pew Research Center tabulations of the 2010 and 2015 American Community Surveys (IPUMS)

How do we choose who is admitted now?

Currently, roughly two-thirds are admitted because they have family members already here. Of the remaining third, about half are admitted based on their job skills and half are refugees from political or religious persecution. There is a backlog of 3.6 million people waiting to have their immigration applications evaluated and processed.

Has the share of population that is foreign born increased?

In 1970, slightly less than 5 percent of the US population was foreign born; today, it is about 13.6 percent.

How many undocumented immigrants live in the United States?

An estimated 10.5 million people now living in the United States entered without permission, typically crossing the border illegally or staying here after their visas have expired. Many have lived in the United States for decades and have spouses and children who are US citizens.

Who are the "DREAMers"?

About 690,000 young people, sometimes known as the "DREAMers," were brought to the United States as children, many as infants or toddlers. A government program called Deferred Action for Childhood Arrivals (DACA) granted them temporary legal status, but that program continues to be at issue.

How has the coronavirus pandemic affected immigration?

Shortly after the first US cases of COVID-19 were reported, the United States closed land borders to nonessential travel, suspended asylum programs, and "paused" processing for those seeking work visas, all but shutting immigration down. The pandemic also has affected immigrants already in the United States. An estimated six million immigrants worked on the front lines of the coronavirus response, in hospitals, in meat-processing plants, and on farms.

Behind all these numbers is a maze of complicated quotas, shifting criteria, and unknowable timelines. The average wait time for a "green card"—which allows permanent legal residence—is about six years. But a family member from the Philippines or Mexico, countries that have millions of applicants, could wait 20 years. In the employment category, someone from India who arrives in the United States on a temporary-worker visa today faces an astonishing 50-year wait for permanent status.

Status of Immigrants in the United States

Foreign-born population estimates, 2017

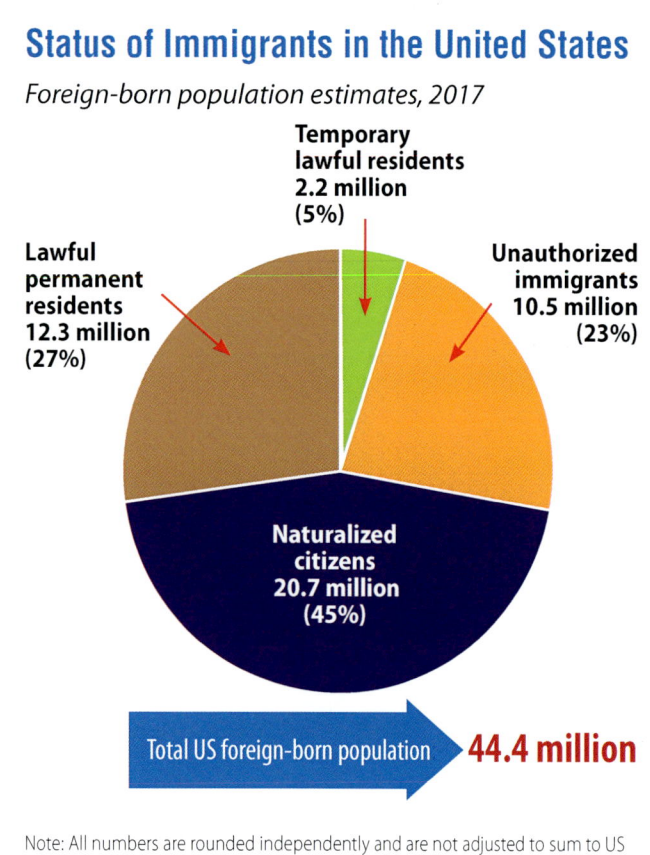

Temporary lawful residents 2.2 million (5%)

Lawful permanent residents 12.3 million (27%)

Unauthorized immigrants 10.5 million (23%)

Naturalized citizens 20.7 million (45%)

Total US foreign-born population → **44.4 million**

Note: All numbers are rounded independently and are not adjusted to sum to US total or other totals.

Source: Pew Research Center estimates for 2017 based on the augmented American Community Survey (IPUMS)

Apprehensions by US Border Patrol at Southwest Border

Total Apprehensions/Inadmissables

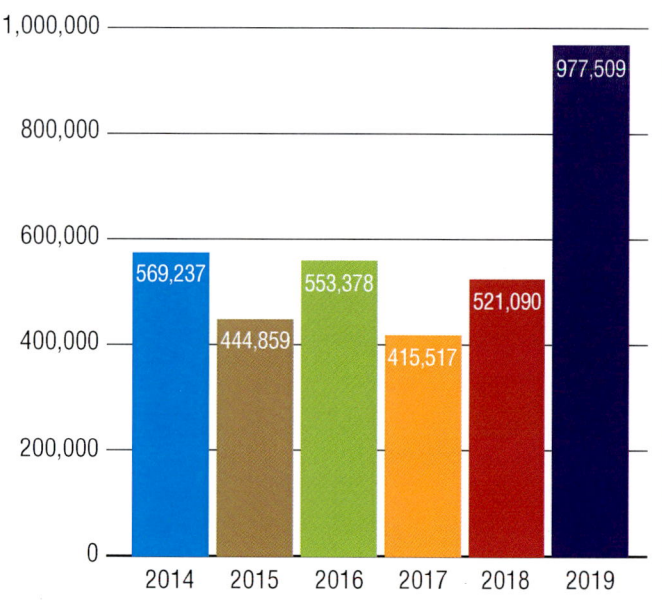

Year	Apprehensions
2014	569,237
2015	444,859
2016	553,378
2017	415,517
2018	521,090
2019	977,509

Source: US Customs and Border Protection

The immigration issue affects all Americans in one way or another. With US birthrates falling, American companies have long experienced a shortage of both high-skilled professionals and low-wage workers. And, while some communities are thriving with large immigrant populations, others question whether their communities will be able to assimilate a growing share of newcomers. These and other challenges raise pressing questions about the nation's immigration policies:

■ Should we reduce the number of immigrants legally admitted into the United States each year? If so, what should we do about worker shortages?

■ How should we handle undocumented immigrants in a way that is humane but also fair to the millions who are waiting to enter legally?

■ Does the current flow of newcomers compromise our sense of national unity or instead build on a rich history of diversity?

■ Does the United States have a humanitarian responsibility to take in refugees whose lives are in danger? How many can we realistically accommodate?

This issue guide offers a framework for considering the priorities that should inform our nation's immigration laws. It presents three options for moving forward, each based on a different way of looking at the issue and each with a different set of prescriptions about what should be done.

None of these options is more "correct" than the others, and each option has trade-offs, risks, or drawbacks that need to be considered if we are to build a fair immigration system that reflects what we hold most valuable.

Option 1:
Welcome Immigrants; Be a Beacon of Freedom

THIS OPTION SAYS THAT IMMIGRATION HAS HELPED MAKE THE US WHAT IT IS TODAY— a dynamic and diverse culture, an engine of the global economy, and a beacon of freedom around the world. It says that part of what defines us as a nation is the opportunity for all to pursue the American dream. We should develop an immigration policy that builds on that tradition by welcoming newcomers, helping immigrant families stay together, and protecting those fleeing war and oppression.

Welcoming immigrants is the right thing to do, according to this option, and it benefits our culture and our economy. The immigration system should be one that reflects the decency and compassion of our nation. Families should stay together. People should be treated humanely.

To remain competitive, we need newcomers who are willing to contribute their talents to strengthening our culture of ingenuity

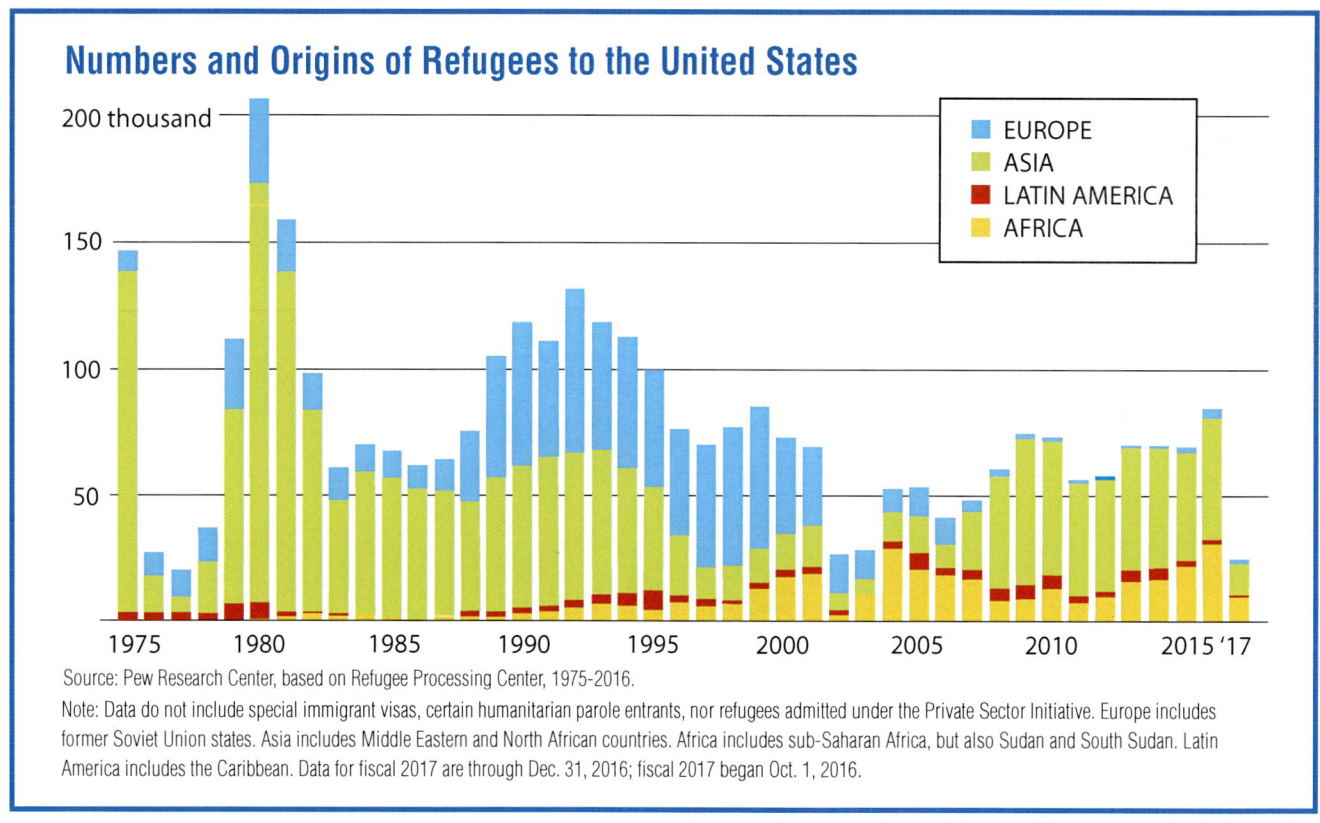

Numbers and Origins of Refugees to the United States

200 thousand

150

100

50

EUROPE
ASIA
LATIN AMERICA
AFRICA

1975   1980   1985   1990   1995   2000   2005   2010   2015 '17

Source: Pew Research Center, based on Refugee Processing Center, 1975-2016.

Note: Data do not include special immigrant visas, certain humanitarian parole entrants, nor refugees admitted under the Private Sector Initiative. Europe includes former Soviet Union states. Asia includes Middle Eastern and North African countries. Africa includes sub-Saharan Africa, but also Sudan and South Sudan. Latin America includes the Caribbean. Data for fiscal 2017 are through Dec. 31, 2016; fiscal 2017 began Oct. 1, 2016.

and entrepreneurship and who are willing to take on jobs, often tough, back-breaking jobs, where there are shortages.

Historically, many of this country's greatest innovations, such as the scientific breakthroughs of Albert Einstein and the inventions of Alexander Graham Bell, were made by immigrants. This is no less true today. According to *Newsweek* magazine, immigrants or their children, including Google's Sergey Brin and Tesla's Elon Musk, founded 45 percent of Fortune 500 companies. Untold millions of smaller businesses, the engines of American growth, were founded by immigrants.

Using US Census and Bureau of Labor Statistics information, the nonprofit group New American Economy found there were over 3.2 million foreign-born entrepreneurs in the United States; they generated $6 trillion in business income in 2018. The immigrants who flourish in the US do not just make better lives for themselves and their families; studies show they generate employment opportunities, contribute to the well-being of communities, replenish our aging population, and have a positive effect on the US economy over the long run.

In some industries, such as farming, fishing, health

care, and construction, immigrants make up for workforce shortages. Almost 30 percent of all physicians and 38 percent of home health aides are immigrants, according to the Migration Policy Institute. Immigrants made up a significant share of workers cleaning hospital rooms, staffing grocery stores, and producing food on the front lines of the pandemic.

Strict quotas and requirements exclude the vast majority of people who apply for admission. And for those who do qualify, red tape and backlogs mean that applications often take years or even decades. The State Department reports that in 2019, there were 3.5 million people on family waiting lists and 125,988 waiting for work visas.

This option says we should honor our historical commitment to immigrants trying to reunite with their families and take part in our unique culture of innovation and entrepreneurship. We have a humanitarian responsibility to people fleeing war and persecution. We need to create a path to citizenship for the millions of immigrants without legal status who already have deep roots in this country. And we need to make sure that those seeking to enter our country are treated humanely no matter what their situation is.

What We Should Do

Create a Path to Legalization for Undocumented Immigrants

This option says that we should create a pathway to citizenship for the United States' 10.5 million undocumented immigrants—that doing so will strengthen our communities, keep families together, and demonstrate our compassion as a nation.

According to the Pew Research Center, about two-thirds of undocumented adults have been in the country at least a decade. The vast majority must provide for their families and live their lives without the support systems that US citizens take for granted.

Some unauthorized immigrants work for cash and never fill out government payroll forms. But most have jobs and pay taxes on their wages, contributing billions of dollars to a system that offers them little or nothing in return. For example, in the most recent accurate review, the Social Security Administration estimates that in 2010 it collected about $13 billion in payroll taxes from undocumented immigrants. Under current laws, such people will not be entitled to any benefits when they retire.

The policies are especially tough for those brought to the United States as children. Sometimes referred to as "DREAMers," these young people have grown up and gone to school here and typically see themselves as American. Some came with parents who entered the country illegally. Others came with parents who entered legally but overstayed their visas. They attend colleges, serve in the military, and own businesses. Yet many also live under constant fear that a deportation order will split their families apart and, for some, force them to return to countries they have no memory of.

There are a number of different proposals for providing a pathway to legal status for undocumented immigrants.

In 1986, President Reagan granted amnesty to about three million immigrants living in the United States without documentation. It was an unpopular decision at the time, but some argue now that this would be the most compassionate and practical action for us today. Others call for a clear pathway to legal status and citizenship, but one that asks immigrants to admit responsibility for breaking the law, pass background and criminal checks, pay penalties and any back taxes they owe, and meet other requirements.

This approach would be in sharp contrast to proposals that call for either high fines or so-called touchback provisions, requiring that people who are here without permission leave the country in order to return on a path to legal status. Given the backlogs and red tape, this would essentially be self-deportation. What we need instead, according to this option, are rules that can bring people out of the shadows and into mainstream society so they can legally work and contribute to the common good.

Seventh-grade teacher Kareli Lizárraga works with her students at STRIVE Prep in Denver, Colorado. She was brought to the United States without documentation as a four-year-old and became an educator thanks to the Deferred Action for Childhood Arrivals (DACA) program.

Accept Immigrants Willing to Meet US Workforce Needs

This option also says that we need to develop an immigration strategy that is responsive to the changing needs of the US economy, making it easier for people from other countries to come to this country to work in industries where their skills are needed. The economy's needs range all the way from high-tech positions to agriculture and hotel service jobs.

Rapidly growing tech companies, for example, depend on temporary work permits—H-1B visas—to recruit globally for skilled math and computer science workers. Demand far exceeds the 85,000 persons annually allowed in on this type of visa. This option says the limits should be substantially changed or even eliminated.

In this view we should also offer green cards to foreign students who have earned graduate degrees from American colleges and universities—especially those in science, technology, engineering, and mathematics—to encourage them to stay here and contribute to the US economy.

We could also create "start-up" visas for foreign entrepreneurs. A small number of visas are reserved for foreign investors, but this would expand the number to include patent holders, business managers, academic researchers, breakthrough scientists, and others with unique contributions to make in the 21st-century knowledge economy.

The US economy also depends on workers who can fill labor shortages in fields such as agriculture, food preparation, and personal care. American families across the country tell stories about grandparents who came here as poor people but managed to work their way into the middle class. This option says we want our immigration system to reflect this heritage.

Accept More Refugees

Honoring our historical commitment to immigrants also means offering refuge to people fleeing war, conflict, and persecution. More people are seeking political asylum now than at any time in history, according to the United Nations.

The United States has traditionally settled more refugees than any other country. But in 2018, that number fell to 22,500, down sharply from a recent high of 97,000 in 2016. The 2020 cap on the number of refugees the US will admit is just 1,800. Perhaps most affected are those fleeing the brutal Syrian civil war, which has generated a humanitarian crisis and millions of refugees. Between limits on refugees and travel bans, the United States admitted just 62 Syrians in 2018, down from 12,587 two years earlier.

Refugee status can be sought only from outside the United States. People who otherwise meet the definition of a refugee but are already here or have arrived at a port of entry can request *asylum*. A crisis developed in 2019 when unprecedented numbers of families with young children began arriving at our southern border, fleeing violence in El Salvador, Guatemala, and Honduras and overwhelming border facilities. Although there are no official limits on numbers of asylum seekers, a "zero tolerance" policy led border officials to separate thousands of children from their families and force others to wait under unsafe conditions across the border for their requests to be processed. Such punishing treatment of vulnerable populations must never be repeated.

This option says that the US has a humanitarian obligation to reduce, or altogether eliminate, these restrictions. The number of refugees in the world dwarfs the number who are resettled, but this option holds that the United States must regain a leadership role in this area.

Trade-offs and Downsides

■ Creating a pathway to citizenship for unauthorized immigrants would have the effect of rewarding people who break the law. It would also be unfair to those who have pursued a legal route to obtaining a green card.

■ Accommodating more immigrants would make the US more diverse and could weaken our sense of national unity and common purpose.

■ Welcoming more refugees could increase national security risks posed by terrorists and other criminals and divert resources from the millions of vulnerable Americans who need help.

■ Hiring more college graduates, entrepreneurs, and even less skilled workers from other countries could mean fewer jobs for unemployed American workers.

Questions for deliberation . . .

1 If we do not strictly guard our borders and enforce our immigration laws, will that tempt more people to come into the country illegally?

2 Many people born in the United States lost their jobs during the pandemic. Should we focus on their needs and potential rather than giving so much attention to recruiting people from other countries?

3 Should the wish to join family members already in the United States be the main reason for admitting new immigrants? How does this help our economy? Does this make us safer?

Option 2:
Enforce the Law; Be Fair to Those Who Follow the Rules

THIS OPTION SAYS WE NEED A FAIR SYSTEM, IN WHICH THE RULES ARE CLEAR AND, ABOVE ALL, ENFORCED. With an estimated 10.5 million people living in the country illegally, our current system is unjust and uncontrolled. In fairness to the long lines of people who are waiting to come to the US legally, we must strengthen our commitment to border security, crack down on visa overstays, and introduce more stringent measures to deal with immigrants living here without authorization.

The United States was founded as "a nation of laws, not of men," in John Adams' famous words. Yet over the last quarter century, we have allowed millions of people to live and work in the United States illegally. According to the Pew Research Center, the number of unauthorized immigrants living in the United States has grown from 3.5 million in 1990 to 10.5 million in 2019 although rates have slowed in recent years.

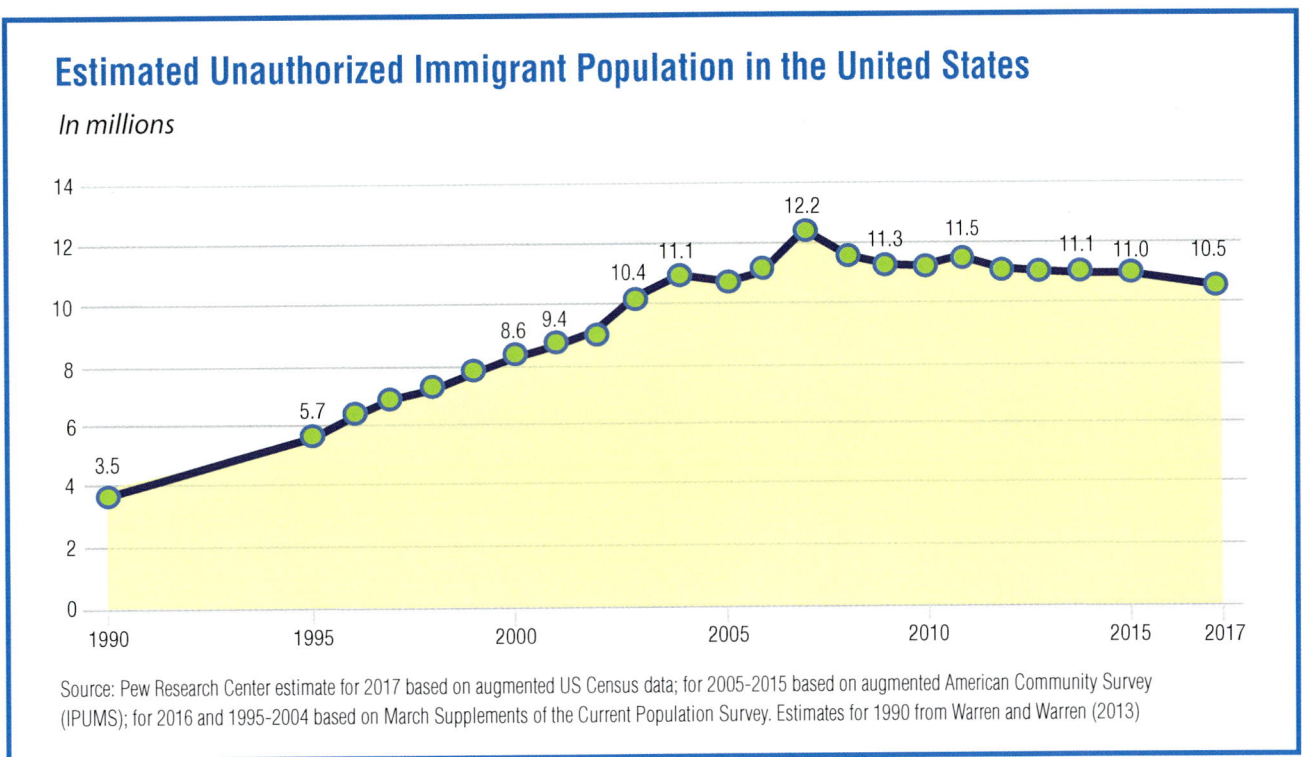

Estimated Unauthorized Immigrant Population in the United States

In millions

Data points: 3.5 (1990), 5.7 (1995), 8.6, 9.4, 10.4, 11.1, 12.2, 11.3, 11.5, 11.1, 11.0, 10.5 (2017)

Source: Pew Research Center estimate for 2017 based on augmented US Census data; for 2005-2015 based on augmented American Community Survey (IPUMS); for 2016 and 1995-2004 based on March Supplements of the Current Population Survey. Estimates for 1990 from Warren and Warren (2013)

Ever since the nation's first immigration policies were put into place, the premise has been that admitting newcomers should be done in an orderly way.

According to this option, the first responsibility of a sovereign nation is to control its borders and defend against external threats. It says that keeping the country safe means getting serious about border security—especially the 2,000-mile boundary between the United States and Mexico.

We must also step up enforcement of our immigration laws within the country. The Department of Homeland Security estimates that of 55 million foreign travelers who arrived in the United States during 2018, more than 666,000 were still in the country after their travel or business visas had expired.

Unauthorized immigrants are excluded from nearly all federal assistance programs, with the exception of school meals and family nutrition programs. But even so, unauthorized immigrants can put a strain on the public purse, particularly at the state level. For example, about 45 percent of undocumented immigrants living in the United States have no health insurance, compared to about 10 percent of US-born or naturalized citizens. Because public hospitals are required to provide emergency medical care to all people, regardless of immigration status, those expenses are passed on to all of us in the form of higher health-care costs. No one yet knows the costs of treating uninsured immigrants during the pandemic.

This option insists that we must eliminate what some call "sanctuary cities" and states. These are places where local authorities have said they will not comply with the federal government's rules that would deport people who are here illegally. According to the government's Immigration and Customs Enforcement (ICE) office, this is widespread. Cities such as Baltimore, Philadelphia, Seattle, and others—as well as some states, including California and Connecticut—have policies that call for only limited cooperation with authorities. Some cities have gone further. Newark, New Jersey, for example, does not comply with ICE "detainers," which are orders to hold people in jail so they can be deported. And in other cases, law enforcement officials have stated that they do not plan to cooperate with immigration officials. This option says we should crack down on sanctuary cities that refuse to cooperate with federal immigration agents seeking to locate and deport undocumented immigrants.

What We Should Do

Get Tough on Illegal Immigration

According to this option, the first step in addressing illegal immigration is to deport those who entered the country illegally or who have overstayed their visas. This is the only way to ensure that our immigration laws are respected and to be fair to the millions of people from around the world applying to come here legally. We need an aggressive deportation strategy, one that sends home many, if not most, immigrants who are here without permission. The nation's immigration courts are notoriously slow moving, and immigrants slated for deportation sometimes wait years before their cases are reviewed by a judge. When the court notices arrive in the mail, people may ignore them or go into hiding. This option says we must overhaul the immigration courts and make them much more efficient.

Another important step is to enforce temporary visas. One way is by using technology, such as fingerprint scans, facial recognition programs, and other means to track people who enter and exit the country. Congress called for a system like this in the wake of the 9-11 terrorist attacks. But with 55 million people visiting the country each year on tourist, student, or work visas, the logistical challenges of this "biometric tracking" were immense. To date, the system has been implemented at only a handful of airports and border crossings. According to this option, we should do what it takes to roll that out nationwide.

This option also says that police officers should be allowed to check people's immigration status if they have a reasonable suspicion that they are in the country illegally. To help make this easier, we should expand federal background check programs that help state and local authorities access the immigration history of people who have committed crimes. And we should also cut federal funding—including pandemic economic recovery aid—to sanctuary cities that refuse to cooperate with federal immigration agents.

The border wall runs several miles through a rural area east of Brownsville, Texas, serving to help control the flow of undocumented immigrants crossing the Rio Grande from Mexico. Several places have wide gaps with no gates visible.

Tighten Security

This option says that any attempt to stop illegal immigration will fail unless it is backed up by strict border security. One way to do that is to build a wall along the almost 2,000-mile United States-Mexico border. There are about 650 miles of fences and walls already in place. Another way is to beef up security at airports and border crossings. We should hire more patrol agents and customs officials at ports of entry to more thoroughly screen out potentially dangerous people at the border. New face-recognition technology and computer data systems could also help us screen for high-risk travelers.

Another way to make the border more secure is to deter migrants from coming in the first place. One way to do this would be to reinstate a zero tolerance policy that calls for prosecuting every adult who crosses the border illegally, even those who come with their children. Not only would it be unfair to prosecute only single adults while allowing adults with children to be released on bond, but it would enable adults to use children as a means to slip into the country and indirectly encourage parents to bring minors along on illegal and inherently dangerous border crossings.

Punish Employers Who Hire Workers without Legal Papers

This option insists that we must hold employers accountable for hiring workers who are here illegally, a law that is rarely enforced. In fields that depend heavily on immigrant workers, such as construction, hospitality, and agriculture, there appears to be a somewhat casual approach to following the rules. Undocumented workers can submit forged documents, and employers can just accept them at face value, which is all they are required to do under the law.

If we are serious about cracking down on unauthorized immigration, says this option, we should require employers to use the federal government's E-Verify program or a system like it. E-Verify is a database that enables employers to check on whether a person is eligible to work in the United States by looking at data from the Department of Homeland Security and the Social Security Administration. The program is voluntary in most states, but this option says that it should be mandatory.

Trade-offs and Downsides

■ Deporting anything close to the 10.5 million immigrants who are in this country illegally would tear their families apart, hurt their employers, and fracture the communities in which they live.

■ Stepping up enforcement of immigration laws would drive a wedge between immigrants and law enforcement and compromise public safety by discouraging witnesses from reporting crimes.

■ Cracking down on sanctuary cities undermines local authority, adds to a climate of fear, and drives away the many otherwise law-abiding immigrants who are contributing to society.

■ Prosecuting employers who hire workers without legal work permits could cause chaos in industries that rely heavily on immigrants, such as agriculture and construction. It could drive up costs for food and housing when times are already tough.

Questions for deliberation . . .

1 Should we balance justice with mercy when it comes to people who entered the United States illegally many years ago? How serious a crime is it, after all? Is deportation really a fair punishment?

2 Identifying and deporting undocumented people will cost billions of dollars. Is this really one of the best ways to spend our tax dollars? How will this help our communities recover from the pandemic's economic toll?

3 Should communities with undocumented immigrants living peacefully and productively in their midst be able to protect them without federal interference? Don't people living in sanctuary cities know what is best for their own communities?

Option 3:
Slow Down and Rebuild Our Common Bonds

THIS OPTION RECOGNIZES THAT NEWCOMERS HAVE STRENGTHENED AMERICAN CULTURE IN THE PAST. But after decades of high immigration, the country is now so diverse that we must regain our sense of national purpose and identity. We should have a measured immigration policy— one that reduces the rate of immigration and assists newcomers as they become part of the American community. We need to find ways to accommodate newcomers without compromising our sense of national unity.

A diversity of cultures is a hallmark of American society. We are a people created from many nations, races, and ethnicities. This is reflected in our national motto, *E pluribus unum*—"out of many, one."

Originally, the phrase referred to the act of political union by which the colonies joined to form a sovereign state. It also aptly describes the enduring tension in the US between our characteristic diversity and our sense of common identity.

The American naturalization ceremony expresses a two-way commitment. We agree to accept and welcome new immigrants as American citizens, with all the rights citizenship conveys, and new citizens agree to become part of this culture, which is why new applicants for citizenship are tested on their knowledge of the Constitution.

This option says that the country is now so diverse that we are losing our sense of shared purpose and national unity. As the late historian Arthur Schlesinger Jr. said, "We've got too much *pluribus* and not enough *unum*."

Over the last five decades, the immigrant population in the United States has expanded dramatically. In 1970, just 4.7 percent of the population was foreign born. Today, the number of foreign-born residents has reached 44.5 million, or 13.6 percent. This rise can be attributed in large part to the 1965 Immigration and Nationality Act, which increased not only the number, but also the diversity, of newcomers. The law eliminated the use of national-origin quotas and replaced it with a "family preference" system for lawful immigration. Today, family reunification accounts for two-thirds of new immigrants.

This option holds that such increased diversity can weaken the fabric of society and compromise our sense of common purpose. According to studies by Harvard political scientist Robert Putnam, people tend to be less charitable and trusting of each other when they perceive that large segments of the population do not look or talk like them. Increased diversity tends to reduce trust and cooperation not only between different racial and ethnic groups, but—surprisingly—also among people of the same race and ethnicity.

This option makes the case for a measured immigration policy that strengthens our common bonds. In practical terms, this means continuing a recent downward trend in admissions, emphasizing integration, and making sure that we can accommodate newcomers without losing the shared values that define who we are as a people.

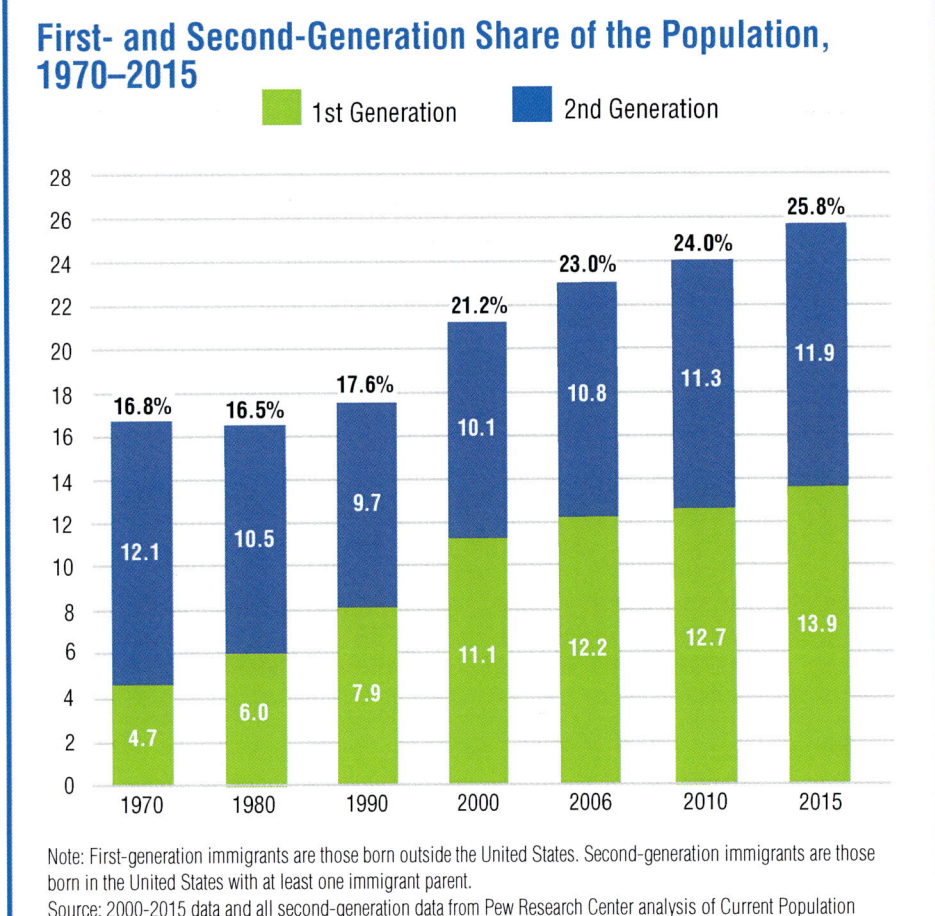

First- and Second-Generation Share of the Population, 1970–2015

1st Generation   2nd Generation

Note: First-generation immigrants are those born outside the United States. Second-generation immigrants are those born in the United States with at least one immigrant parent.
Source: 2000-2015 data and all second-generation data from Pew Research Center analysis of Current Population Surveys (IPUMS); historical trend from Passel and Cohn (2008) and Edmundsoton and Passel (1994)

What We Should Do

Restrict the Number of Immigrants Legally Admitted into the United States

For the last decade, the United States admitted about one million people a year as legal immigrants. This option proposes that this number is too high and that it strains our ability to welcome and absorb newcomers as we have in the past. There are a number of ways to reduce this number.

Under current law, US citizens can sponsor spouses, minor children, parents, siblings, and adult married children to enter the United States. Green-card holders who are not US citizens can also sponsor relatives, including spouses, minor children, and adult unmarried children. One way to rein in immigration would be to limit family-based green cards to spouses and young children. Another would be to give preference to immigrants who already speak English and have other skills or education levels needed by our workforce.

This option also says we should eliminate the program introduced in 1990 that offers citizens of countries with low immigration rates a chance to "win" a green card. This "diversity lottery" confers 50,000 visas per year.

Strengthen the Integration of Newcomers into Communities

Another step we can take to reinforce our sense of common identity is to help people get established once they arrive from other countries. This is especially true in the case of refugees, who depend on placement agencies—nonprofits such as the International Rescue Committee—to find new homes for them. The agencies usually try to place people in communities where they have family or friends, often concentrating them in a handful of states.

In 2019, for example, a quarter of all refugees arriving in the US settled in one of four states—Texas, Washington, New York, or California, prompting Texas to declare it would not accept any more in 2020. This uneven approach to resettlement means that many refugees remain in immigrant enclaves and never fully assimilate into American culture and society.

This option says immigration agencies should actively oversee the resettlement of new arrivals, making sure refugees are more evenly spread out and better integrated into communities, rather than leaving it up to community organizations and nonprofits.

Some places have experimented with new and promising community approaches to helping immigrants get settled and become actively engaged in communities. The benefits of these programs often extend beyond immigrants themselves to the community as a whole, resulting in new jobs, economic development, and other positive outcomes. In Pittsburgh, for example, city leaders have created a program to attract "asylum artists"—individuals who encourage cross-cultural exchange and bring new vibrancy to older

Refugee Elizabeth Alier from South Sudan (right) works with volunteer Jessie Dotson on doll faces during an advanced sewing circle meeting, a Friends of Refugees program, in Clarkston, Georgia. The women in the group, who are from from Iraq, Bhutan, Burundi, Sudan, and South Sudan, sell their dolls and aprons on Etsy. Refugee resettlement programs have identified Clarkston as a good fit for displaced persons of many backgrounds.

neighborhoods. Artists are provided with spaces to freely express themselves through public art displays, cultural events, and a journal publication.

Promote English as Our Common Language

This option recognizes that speaking a common language is a powerful unifying influence. Strengthening the role of English in US society and requiring that newcomers learn the language could go a long way toward integrating our diverse immigrant communities. Current law requires people applying for US citizenship to demonstrate proficiency in English, but not those applying for green cards.

This option holds that we should give preference to immigrants who have learned English and make learning our language a requirement for lawful permanent residence here.

This may place a burden on some immigrants—refugees, for example—and hurt American employers who depend on foreign-born workers, but it would help new-comers thrive in our communities, join in our activities, and give them more opportunities and independence.

There are additional steps we could take to consolidate the role of English as our common language. For instance, we could require that elected officials and government employees conduct all business in English. The intent would not be to ban other languages, but rather to foster and support the language all Americans share.

A further action along these lines would be for public schools to develop English immersion programs that teach all subjects in English and place newcomers in classrooms with native English speakers. Immigrant children will pick up their new language more quickly while also learning about American culture and democratic values. A trend in the 1980s and 1990s was to offer dual instruction in English and other languages, which is expensive and may hinder, rather than enhance, students' ability to become fluent English speakers.

Trade-offs and Downsides

■ Restricting immigration might hurt our future workforce—and threaten our economy—by further lowering the national birthrate, which is driven by higher immigrant births.

■ Limiting family migration will split apart many immigrant families.

■ Emphasizing national unity and common identity will favor those in the majority and make it harder for racial, ethnic, and cultural minority groups to be accepted into the dominant culture.

■ Immersing newcomers in English can be traumatic for adults and adolescents who don't pick up new languages as easily as young children do. Older students are likely to fall behind in their other subjects, impeding their overall education.

Questions for deliberation . . .

1 Is immigration really responsible for the loss of unity we see in our country today? Are there other factors that are more to blame for these divisions?

2 Most immigrants are hard working, family oriented, and grateful to be in the United States. Given the numbers of immigrants who served on the front lines of the pandemic, will our communities really be better off with fewer of them? What will we lose if skilled, talented, and hard-working immigrants start going elsewhere?

3 Industries such as agriculture and construction keep prices down by relying on low-wage immigrant workers. Will we accept the rising costs that come from paying higher salaries to US workers? Won't higher food and housing costs just make life harder for working families already reeling from the economic collapse caused by the pandemic?

Closing Reflections

ACTING ON THE IDEAS AND PROPOSALS presented here will bring about changes that affect all of us, in every city and town—those of us who are citizens and those of us who are not. It is important to think carefully about what matters most to us and what kinds of decisions and actions will enable our communities and our country to thrive.

Before ending the forum, take some time to revisit some of the central questions this issue guide raises:

- Should we strictly enforce the law and deport people who are here without permission, or would deporting millions of people outweigh their crime?

- Should we welcome more newcomers to build a more vibrant and diverse society, or does this pose too great a threat to national unity?

- Should we accept more of the millions of refugees and asylum seekers fleeing gang violence and war, or should we avoid the risk of taking in people whose backgrounds may not have been fully checked?

- Should our priority be to help immigrants assimilate into our distinctively American way of life and insist they learn English, or should we instead celebrate a growing mosaic of different peoples?

Some important questions to consider are these: On what do we agree? About what do we need to talk more? Who else should we hear from? What more do we need to know? How do the ideas and options in this guide affect what we do as individuals, as members of our communities, and as citizens and residents in the United States as a whole?

Summary

Option 1:

Welcome Immigrants; Be a Beacon of Freedom

THIS OPTION SAYS THAT IMMIGRATION HAS HELPED MAKE THE UNITED STATES WHAT IT IS TODAY—a dynamic and diverse culture, an engine of the global economy, and a beacon of freedom around the world. We should develop an immigration policy that builds on that tradition, one that welcomes newcomers, helps immigrant families stay together, and protects those fleeing war and oppression. Welcoming immigrants is not only the right thing to do; it benefits our economy and counters falling US birth rates. To remain competitive in a fast-changing global marketplace, the United States needs newcomers who are willing to contribute their skills to strengthening our culture of ingenuity and entrepreneurship.

A Primary Drawback

This option would add even more burden to systems already overwhelmed by historically high levels of immigration.

ACTIONS	DRAWBACKS
Give those who entered the US without permission years ago a path to legal status. It's time to forgive and welcome these people who have become part of our communities.	This allows immigrants who violated our laws to cut in front of the line of thousands of people who are seeking to enter the United States legally.
Welcome immigrants who are willing to work, whether in low-skilled jobs many Americans do not want or in high-skilled jobs where there are shortages.	Given how the pandemic shutdown has devastated our economy, we should focus on helping our own citizens learn new skills to get better jobs.
Accept more refugees fleeing violence and deprivation in countries such as Syria, El Salvador, and Guatemala. We have a moral obligation to help.	There are US citizens in need, too, and it is difficult to vet people coming from such areas of upheaval.
Provide legal residency and the ability to apply for citizenship to DREAMers, the term commonly used for undocumented immigrants who were brought to the United States as young children.	It's not fair to allow this group to benefit from the illegal actions of their families.
Allow all residents to get driver's licenses regardless of whether they are citizens or not.	This could make it easier for criminals and terrorists to get fake documents.
What else?	**What's the trade-off?**

Summary

Option 2:

Enforce the Law; Be Fair to Those Who Follow the Rules

THIS OPTION SAYS WE NEED A FAIR SYSTEM, IN WHICH THE RULES ARE CLEAR AND, ABOVE ALL, ENFORCED. Ever since the nation's first immigration policies were put into place, the premise has been that welcoming newcomers should be done in an orderly way. But with an estimated 10.5 million people living in the country illegally, our current system is unjust and uncontrolled. In fairness to the many people who are waiting to come to the US and stay here legally, we have an obligation to enforce our borders and deport people who enter the country without our permission. That is why we must strengthen our commitment to border security, crack down on those who overstay their visas, and introduce more stringent measures to deal with immigrants living outside the law.

A Primary Drawback

This will harm millions of people now living in our communities and contributing to our society. It will spread fear in cities and towns nationwide.

ACTIONS	DRAWBACKS
Identify people who entered the country illegally and deport them. Require that they reapply for entry.	This will tear up families—many of which include one or more US-born children. The punishment is not only impractical but far outweighs the crime.
Cut off federal funding, including pandemic economic recovery aid, to sanctuary cities that refuse to cooperate with federal immigration agents.	This punishes entire communities over disputes that should be settled in court. It could mean underfunded police departments and schools in some places and deny aid at a time of dire need.
Prosecute employers if they hire workers without legal papers.	This will create chaos in industries such as agriculture and construction and lead to higher prices for basic goods such as food and housing when times are already tough.
Build a secure southern border wall.	This will cost billions of tax dollars needed instead for pandemic recovery. Plus, it fails to address problems with people entering from Canada or through airports or people over-staying temporary visas.
Detain all adults who enter the country illegally even if this means separating families.	Such a zero tolerance policy traumatizes children who had no say in their parents' decisions and invites international condemnation.
What else?	**What's the trade-off?**

Summary

Option 3:

Slow Down and Rebuild Our Common Bonds

THIS OPTION RECOGNIZES THAT NEWCOMERS HAVE STRENGTHENED OUR CULTURE IN THE PAST. But the number of foreign-born residents has reached 44.4 million, or 13.6 percent of the population. Fifty years ago, the foreign-born share of our population was 4.7 percent. The country is now so diverse that we must regain our sense of national purpose and identity. We need to moderate the flow of immigrants and focus more on helping newcomers integrate into US society. We should have a measured immigration policy—one that reduces the rate of immigration and ensures that immigrants become part of the US community. We need to find ways to accommodate newcomers without compromising our sense of national unity.

A Primary Drawback

This option would rob us of much of the energy and hard work people from around the world bring to the United States. The coronavirus pandemic only underscored how many of our "essential workers"—serving in hospitals, staffing grocery stores, and producing food—are immigrants.

ACTIONS	DRAWBACKS
Reduce the number of legal immigrants admitted to the United States each year.	This deprives us of the workers needed in key industries such as agriculture and construction and could threaten the economy by lowering birthrates.
Give preference to immigrants who already speak English.	This would place an undue burden on some immigrants—especially those who are willing to take on some of the back-breaking jobs most Americans do not want.
Restrict family reunification to spouses and young children, and concentrate on admitting immigrants who will work in areas where we need them.	This would split immigrant families apart, forcing people who come here to leave loved ones behind, sometimes in danger or poverty.
Schools should require English immersion programs so newcomers learn the language as quickly as possible and absorb US culture and democratic values.	Special language programs take needed time and funds away from other important subjects. Besides, teaching classes in both languages would better prepare students to participate in today's global economy.
Distribute refugees among many communities so they are not all resettled in the same few places, which overburdens the communities' ability to absorb them and provide the support they need.	This would require more communities to accept and welcome newcomers.
What else?	**What's the trade-off?**

The National Issues Forums

The National Issues Forums (NIF) is a network of organizations that bring together citizens around the nation to talk about pressing social and political issues of the day. Thousands of community organizations—including schools, libraries, churches, civic groups, and others—have held forums designed to give people a public voice in the affairs of their communities and their nation.

Forum participants engage in deliberation, which is simply weighing options for action against things held commonly valuable. This calls upon them to listen respectfully to others, sort out their views in terms of what they most value, consider courses of action and their disadvantages, and identify areas of common ground for action.

Issue guides like this one are designed to support these conversations. They present varying perspectives on the issue at hand, suggest actions to address identified problems, and note the trade-offs of taking those actions to remind participants that all solutions have costs as well as benefits.

In this way, forum participants move from holding individual opinions to making collective choices as members of a community—the kinds of choices from which public policy may be forged or public action may be taken at community as well as national levels.

Forum Questionnaire

If you participated in this forum, please fill out a questionnaire, which is included in this issue guide or can be accessed online at **www.nifi.org/questionnaires**. If you are filling out the enclosed questionnaire, please return the completed form to your moderator or to the National Issues Forums Institute, 100 Commons Road, Dayton, Ohio 45459.

If you moderated this forum, please fill out a Moderator Response sheet, which is online at **www.nifi.org/questionnaires**.